Contents

Introduction

Divali, known the world over as the 'festival of light', is an annual celebration of spirituality. It encapsulates all that the exotic and fascinating world of Hinduism has to offer. Evolving over thousands of years in India and popularised in the West since the 1960s in the form of the New Age Movement, this global religion has captured the hearts and minds of hundreds of millions of people from all cultures and on all continents.

This book relates the experiences of five devoted Hindus whose search for truth led them to amazing encounters with God both in India and in other parts of the world. Journey with them through a rich tapestry of colours, rituals, emotions and beliefs as they seek the ultimate light.

CHAPTER 1

Destined for Royalty

Anand Chaudhari
India

Anand Chaudhari descended from a long line of famous Hindu Brahmin priests in Goa, India. His father, Sushi Kumar Chaudhari, who took the title 'Shastri' – one who has mastered the Hindu Scriptures – was the chief priest of the temple called the Shri Santadurga, one of the Kashmiri Brahmins' three most important places of worship in Goa. Sushi Kumar frequently travelled throughout India lecturing leading Hindus on their sacred writings.

In 1939 an outbreak of smallpox decimated Goa's population, taking four of Anand's brothers in death. The disease struck Anand himself, an experience that remained vivid in his mind for the rest of his life. In his own words:

"One night my father sat at my bedside and, seeing my life slipping away, from the depths of his heart he prayed to God, a God he did not even know. I remember that prayer. My father promised that if God would spare me, I would be given to Him for His service. He doubtless meant this to be as a Hindu priest, but how differently God answered. He did hear that prayer, and I recovered."

With many millions of different gods worshipped in India, Sushi Kumar's prayer seemed somewhat unusual. Perhaps

4

somewhere in the back of his mind he believed in a supreme deity yet unknown to him. After the death of his four sons, Anand's father sank into deep depression. What terrible sins had he committed in his former life to inflict such a heavy karma? At times the guilt seemed unbearable. What acts of penance could possibly expiate all the evils of his past life? Other than performing the necessary regular priestly functions in the temple, Sushi Kumar withdrew into Yoga, meditation and the endless recitation of mantras, especially the word 'OM' (or 'AUM'), which represents Brahman, the impersonal force of the universe.

Determined not to renege on his promise to God, Sushi Kumar began to train his son Anand in the disciplines of the Hindu priesthood. Under the tutelage of his father and other priests, Anand studied the sacred writings of the Vedas, Upanishads, Bhagavad-Gita and Ramayana. He learnt how to calculate and construct astrological charts, how to practise Yoga and meditation and how to perform priestly rituals, especially those connected with the goddess Durga, the wife of Shiva, the focus of worship in the Shri Santadurga temple.

Anand memorised endless religious instructions and mantras. The mantras he used as a magical force to 'enchain the power of the gods', to cure or cause disease, to act as a preservative or destructive force, and to cause or erase the effects of spirit possession. One mantra, the famous 'gayatri', reads: "*Let us worship the supreme light of the sun, the god of all things, who can so well guide our understanding like an eye suspended in the vault of heaven.*"

Some priests recite the gayatri as many as 1,000 or even 5,000 times a day hoping for the remission of their sins, or to gain wealth, health or happiness. Anand's training also featured warnings. One read: "*Remember, O my son, that there is only one God who is the Creator, Lord and source of all things, whom every Brahmin*

5

should worship in secret. But know also that this is a great mystery that must never be revealed to the vulgar and ignorant people. Should you ever reveal it, surely great misfortune will fall upon you."

His father intended for Anand to gain a good all-round education to further facilitate his priestly calling, so in 1942 he sent him to Bombay (Mumbai) where he stayed with his wealthy uncle and aunt. Throughout his time at school and later at university he never ceased performing his priestly duties. Anand's life was nothing if not busy. At Bombay University Anand took a degree course in philosophy. At the time it was fashionable for students to join the growing Communist movement and, seeing no serious contradiction between the priesthood and a communistic political outlook, Anand signed up. His local Communist organization asked him to run classes for the labouring people in a slum area of Bombay. The experience raised disturbing questions in Anand's mind.

"I visited where the labourers lived. I saw their squalid conditions, fifteen or sixteen people living in a one room shack. There was no running water, no sanitation facilities. The people who had jobs worked like animals for a few cents a day. Hinduism seemed to be always looking back. All you have in this life is a result of fulfilling your karma – what you have done in your past life – and whatever you are doing now will determine your next birth. The Harijan (outcaste) does what he is expected to do, and the Brahmin does what is predestined for him."

As a priest, Anand enjoyed the respect of his local community which frequently called upon him to offer special pujas (ritual sacrifices), to officiate at weddings and cremations and to appease the gods in times of trouble. Privately however, he was becoming increasingly uneasy with the entire belief system of Hinduism. He began to feel that its structure had been deliberately designed to favour and safeguard the rights and privileges of the minority Brahmin ruling class. At the opposite end of the unjust caste system were the hopelessly enfeebled and unfortunate majority, whose belief in reincarnation kept them quiet with the hope of future betterment if they submitted to the religious order and lived good lives. Later Anand reflected:

"What was the purpose of their endless sacrifices and daily rituals? The gods simply locked them into their wretchedness, to live their miserable existence without complaint – to suffer pain to its numbness, to give something out of their nothing, to appease the gods' anger so that perchance they would return in the next life as a man rather than a woman, or a farmer rather than a barber?"

Even Anand's political fervour began to wane. For three years he had readily devoured anything communistic. He had even spoken at Communist rallies. Yet his heart ached with a feeling of emptiness. Disillusionment overwhelmed him as he read the works of several ex-Communists. Then came a turning point.

One night in 1953, the Bombay Communist Party asked Anand to speak at a student debate. His pro-Communist speech drew enthusiastic applause from the audience but when his opponent, a student called Joseph, rose to reply, Anand was in for a shock. Joseph's final words were: *"According to my faith, peace will come in this world only when Jesus Christ comes back to establish His kingdom on earth – and not until then."*

Anand was aghast. Jesus Christ? What could that Western god have to do with peace on earth, never mind providing solutions to the pain and poverty of India? Yet Joseph's statement refused to go away. It constantly played on Anand's mind.

"I tried to forget what I had heard, but I couldn't. That name seemed to be hooked into my mind and I could not shake it loose. Then it struck me.

7

I had studied just about everything else; why not see what this was all about? So about ten days after the debate I contacted Joseph to find out where I could read more about Jesus Christ."

When the two students met Anand found that Joseph could not fully answer all his questions.

"*Read the Bible, especially the Gospels,*" Joseph said, "*God will talk to you and show you the truth.*"

Anand took up the challenge. His thoughtful examination of the words of Jesus left him feeling overawed by the power, majesty and love contained in them. Nothing he recalled in the Hindu religion came close to the teachings of Christ.

"*I read through Matthew and the other Gospels,*" says Anand, "*Much I didn't understand, but I was like parched ground soaking up life-giving water.*"

For months he agonised over the gospels, struck by the purity he found in Christ in stark contrast to the immoral and capricious gods of his own religion. He remembered the god Shiva who in a fit of jealousy killed his own son Ganesha by decapitation and replaced his head with the head of an elephant; and the goddess Kali who drinks human blood and wears a necklace of human skulls. As he compared the Hindu gods with Jesus Christ he began to entertain the possibility that Jesus might actually be the true God after all. Yet he also entertained another possibility – what if, as some of the Gurus like Ramakrishna had said, Kali, Rama, Hanuman, Jesus and all the gods, are all able to lead to enlightenment? Yet the more Anand read the gospels, the more convinced he became that he could not mix Jesus together with the gods of Hinduism, most especially since Jesus claimed to be the only path to God, stating: "*I am the Way, the Truth and the*

8

Life. No one comes to the Father except through Me" (John 14:6). In another passage the Bible stated: "*There is one God and one mediator between God and men, the man Christ Jesus who gave Himself a ransom for all.*" (1 Tim 2:5-6)

Anand eventually became convinced of the impossibility of coating his Hindu foundation and Communist superstructure with a new layer of Christianity. Through reading the Bible Anand also became aware of his guilt and sinfulness before a pure and holy God. To a Hindu priest and teacher the idea of being a 'sinner' was repulsive. In Anand's own words: "*I never felt myself as a guilty sinner before. According to Hindu philosophy I was completely all right.*"

As the days passed by cracks began to appear in Anand's philosophical edifice. Finally, after a long struggle, both intellectually and emotionally, Anand visited his favourite spot by the sea on 23rd January 1954. He had come to an end of his posturing and self-righteousness. Falling on his knees he cast himself on the mercy of God, pleading for forgiveness through the Lord Jesus and surrendering His life to the service of the one true God. The Lord gave him real assurance of the answer to his desperate call:

"*I will never forget that experience. I felt such a peace in my heart that everything else was gone. I felt free and utter joy. All the turmoil ceased – the conflict, everything – I was left with just a serene peace, calm and quietness. I experienced my sins being forgiven in a personal way by the only true and holy God through the death of Jesus on the cross. Because He had risen from the dead, He was alive and had given me eternal life. I wanted to tell everyone I met what had happened to me.*"

Before leaving the beach he removed his priestly Brahmin chord, flinging it as far as he could into the sea. Joyful though he was, the fact is becoming a true Christian was not a soft option for Anand. His change of heart had come after long consideration of the issues involved and there was a price to pay. He took the opportunity to break the news to his relatives at a family reunion at his uncle's house in Bombay. Anand's claim to have met God through Jesus was too much for his father.

"Impossible!" his father retorted, *"The ancient monks spent many years in meditation to gain this experience. Even I have never had it, though I've sought it all my life. How could you, a mere boy, have such an experience?"*

"But it's true father," Anand replied, *"I've been seeking truth for a long time. I even joined the Communists at the university for a time, but they have no morality. Then I began to study the Christian scriptures, and there I found the true holy God – Jesus Christ."*

After an angry outburst, Anand's father lapsed into a stony silence until Anand left Bombay to return home. Tragedy followed shortly afterwards. The next month Anand's parents attended the Kumbh Mela festival at the River Ganges. According to Hindu astrologers, uniquely special powers, only manifested once every 144 years, were to be at work in the sacred river in 1954, enabling the shortening of the devotees' rebirth cycle by 1,000 years. An estimated two to four million people crowded into an 80 acre area by the Ganges hoping for healing, forgiveness and deliverance from the cycle of reincarnation. As the crowd surged forward, Anand's parents and many others were crushed to death. Adding to his overwhelming grief, Anand's relatives blamed the tragic deaths on Anand's conversion to Christ. They saw it as a punishment from the gods and Anand was exiled from the family.

Later he went to a Bible school in Jhansi in the province of Uttar Pradesh where he studied the Bible under Christian lecturers. Now married, Anand preaches the good news of Jesus Christ in various parts of India. He occasionally reflects on the promise his father made at his side while he lay at death's door with smallpox as a child. Could he see him again Anand would assure him:

"Father, I have honoured your promise. I have served God, the only true God, with all my being. He has blessed me far beyond your deepest desires, for I was destined to serve the King of Kings."

CHAPTER 2

Death of a Guru

Rabindranath Maharaj
India

Rabindranath Maharaj entered the world with a long and proud history behind him. His family tree read like a who's who of Brahmin priests. Growing up in the West Indies he trained as a Yogi, following as was expected in the footsteps of his famous father for whom many Hindus claimed avatar status – one of the great gods living on earth. Rabi's father was treated like the other household gods being washed, dressed and fed daily. His admirers claimed he had experienced the bliss of Nirvana thereby escaping the seemingly endless cycle of reincarnation. Yet although Rabi admired his father, his incredible spirituality put a strain on his relationship with his son. In Rabi's own words:

"Because of the vows he had taken before I was born, not once did my father ever speak to me or pay me the slightest heed. Just two words from him would have made me unspeakably happy. More than anything else in the whole world I wanted to hear him say, 'Rabi! Son!' Just once. But he never did.

"For eight long years he uttered not a word, not even a whispered confidence to my mother. The trance-like state which he had achieved through Yoga used to be considered peculiar by those unacquainted with eastern mysticism. However, 'altered states of consciousness' have gained acceptance in the West, through hypnotherapy, autosuggestion, guided imagery, Yoga, T.M.

and visualisation. My father was the ultimate example in real life of what the Yogis and gurus, now famous in Europe and America, teach. He lived what they talk about, as few men ever have.

"*No-one, not even my mother, ever knew the exact vows he had taken; they could only be surmised. Sitting in the lotus position, the toes of both feet turned up on top of his knees, on the board that he also used for a bed, he passed his days in meditation and the reading of the sacred scripture. Nothing else. Mantras (repeated Hindu prayers) are considered a necessity for meditation, creating vibrations that attract deities. But my father was even beyond the use of mantras. We all considered him to be in direct communion with Brahman. So completely had he turned within to realise the true Self that he never acknowledged any human presence, although admirers came from miles around to worship him and to lay before him their offerings of fruit and flowers, cotton, cloth and money. No one ever aroused a response from him. He seemed to be in another world.*

"*Even as a small boy, a fierce pride stirred within me whenever I heard my father praised. With awe and respect, religious Hindus spoke of him as one who had the courage and conviction to tread higher and mysterious paths. In the opinion of many, including the greatest pundit (expert in Hinduism) I ever knew, my Father was an avatar. I heard that word for many years before I really understood what it meant. How good it sounded — and so very special! I knew that I was special too, because he was my father. One day I would also be a great Yogi.*"

Then tragedy struck. Rabi's father died. His stiff body was placed on a great pile of firewood and sacrificed to Agni the god of fire. Standing nearby, Rabi's mother somehow found strength to follow the teaching of Krishna: she would mourn neither the living nor the dead. Not once did she cry as the flames consumed her husband's body. Rabi's father was widely mourned and sadly missed especially by Rabi who soon suffered another crushing blow. Shortly after her husband's death, Rabi's devout Hindu mother left their home in Trinidad, West Indies, to go to India to scatter her husband's ashes on the river Ganges (which is also worshipped as a god). She did not return to see her son for many years, choosing instead to pursue a career in Yoga. She eventually became one of the top Yoga instructors both in India and the Caribbean.

Despite the double shock of losing his father and his mother, Rabi remained determined to become a guru. He moved to live at his grandmother's spacious house. (His grandfather had died of a heart attack when Rabi was still young). Rabi says:

"*Nana* [Rabi's grandfather] *had been heavily involved in Hindu occultism and was critical of those who merely philosophised about their religion without learning to use their supernatural forces. As I grew older, Ma* [Rabi's grandmother] *confided in me about a secret she had kept in her heart for years and had shared only with Aunt Revati: that Nana had sacrificed his first son as an offering to one of his favourite gods. This was not an uncommon practice, but it was never spoken about openly. Nana's favourite deity was Lakshmi, a goddess of wealth and prosperity and consort of Vishnu the preserver, who demonstrated her great powers when Nana rose at almost one leap to become one of the most powerful and wealthy men in my native Trinidad. When the small frame shack that Nana had built for his family and business mysteriously burned down, he replaced it with a huge house that became a landmark on the road from Port of Spain to San Fernando. No one could fathom where the money had suddenly come from. Not many of the hundreds of thousands of immigrants from India and their descendants had been able to accumulate wealth so easily and so suddenly. We all believed that powerful gods had helped him. In turn he had given his soul to them.*"

Like his father before him, Hindu priests, holy men and psychics all predicted that Rabi would become a great Hindu. He began his training for the Hindu priesthood at the ashram in

14

Durga under the supervision of a highly respected head priest. Hanuman, Shiva, Krishna, Ganesha and others, including the cow god, became his favourite deities. Rabi's experiences were often intense and deeply spiritual:

"Nothing was more important than our daily transcendental meditation which Krishna advocated as the surest way to eternal bliss. But it could also be dangerous. Frightening psychic experiences awaited the unwary meditator. Demons described in the Vedas (Hindu scriptures) had been known to take possession of some Yogis. 'Kundalini' power (or energy flow) said to be coiled like a serpent at the base of the spine, could produce ecstatic experiences when released in deep meditation – or, if not properly controlled, could do great mental and even bodily harm. The line between ecstasy and horror was very fine. For that reason we initiates were closely supervised by the Brahmacharya (celibate priest) and his assistant.

"During the daily meditation I began to have visions of psychedelic colours, to hear unearthly music and to visit exotic 'planets' where the gods conversed with me, encouraging me to attain even higher states of consciousness. Sometimes in my trance I encountered the same horrible demonic creatures that are depicted in the images in Hindu, Buddhist, Shinto and other religious temples. These were frightful experiences, but the Brahmacharya explained that they were normal and urged me to pursue the quest for self-realization. At times I experienced a sense of mystical unity with the universe. I was the Universe, Lord of all, omnipotent, omnipresent. My instructors were excited about this. I was obviously a chosen vessel, they said, destined for early success in the search for union with Brahman. The forces that had guided my father were now guiding me. Indeed, seated before a mirror I worshipped myself – and why not? I was God. Krishna, in the precious and beautiful Bhagavad-Gita, had promised this divine knowledge to the one who practised Yoga. This was the nectar for the meditators to drink. It wasn't a question of becoming God, but of simply realising who I really was and had been all the time. Walking the streets, I felt that I really was the Lord of the Universe and that my creatures were bowing before me."

Despite Rabi's self-realization he was secretly addicted to cigarettes and regularly stole as a way of life. While on the one hand his 'spirituality' grew deeper and deeper, on the other hand the teenage Rabi recognised himself becoming more and more arrogant, proud and selfish. This contradictory state of affairs was apparently quite widespread. Rabi discovered that numbers of his guru heroes were also living wicked lives.

"It troubled me deeply to see how the state of blissful peace I had reached in meditation could so easily be destroyed by a scolding from my aunt accusing me of laziness or of failing to do my fair share around the house. Normally a peaceful person, at such times my temper would flare and I would use harsh language in defending myself. Once I grabbed Nana's old leather strap with which he had so often beaten the family, and lashed it repeatedly across the backs of several of my younger girl cousins before retreating in confusion and shame.

"Although the peace I experienced in meditation so easily deserted me, the occult forces that my practice of Yoga cultivated and aroused lingered on and began to manifest themselves in public. Knowing that without these displays of the supernatural my following could never be very great, I welcomed this growing spiritual power. Often those who bowed before me would sense a brightness and experience an inner illumination when I touched them on the forehead in bestowal of my blessing. I was only a teenager, but I was already administering the 'Shakti Pat', famous among the gurus and a true mark of the authenticity of my calling. Shakti is one of the names given to Kali, Shiva's murderous, blood-drinking consort, the mother goddess of power who dispenses the primal force flowing at the heart of the universe. How it excited me to become a channel of her power!

"Often while I was in deep meditation the gods seemed to become visible and talked with me. It would be years before I would learn that such experiences were being duplicated in laboratories under the watchful eyes of para-psychologists through the use of hypnosis and LSD. In my Yoga trances

most often I would be alone with Shiva the destroyer, sitting fearfully at his feet, the huge cobra coiled about his neck staring at me, hissing and darting out its tongue threateningly. Sometimes I wondered why none of the gods I ever encountered seemed kind, gentle and loving. But at least they seemed real. I had no doubt about that."

Not until Rabi reached high school did his Hindu beliefs begin to take a few knocks. As a Hindu in a school of mixed religions he occasionally ended up on the receiving end of the mockery of others.

"*Is it true that Hindus believe everything is God?*" asked one boy.

Rabi nodded.

"*You mean a fly is God, or an ant, or a stinkbug?*"

"*You are laughing because you don't understand,*" Rabi retorted. "*You see only the illusion but you don't see the One reality – Brahman.*"

"*Are you God?*" asked a Portuguese boy incredulously.

"*Yes,*" Rabi responded firmly, "*and so are all Hindus. They just need to realise it.*"

"*How are you going to realise what isn't true?*" the boy replied. "*You didn't create the world!*"

An English boy who seemed familiar with Hinduism said to Rabi while winking at his friends, "*I hear you're a vegetarian who doesn't believe in taking any life. Don't you know that even vegetables have the seven characteristics of life? So, vegetarians take life too. How about when you boil water for your tea? Think of all the millions of bacteria you kill then.*"

And so it went on. Although on the outside Rabi was as strong as ever, numerous doubts began to assail him.

"My religion was beautiful in theory, but I was having serious difficulties applying it in everyday life. If there was only one reality, then Brahman was evil as well as good, death as well as life, hatred as well as love. That made everything meaningless, and life became an absurdity. If reason also was 'maya' (an illusion), as the Vedas taught, then how could I trust any concept, including the idea that all was maya and only Brahman was real? If none of my reasonings were to be trusted, how could I be sure that the bliss I sought was not just another illusion. My only hope was Yoga, which Krishna in the Gita promised would dispel all ignorance through the realization that I was none other than God himself."

One day Rabi was about to touch the forehead of a woman who had come for his blessing when he distinctly heard an authoritative voice saying, *"You are not God, Rabi!"* Instinctively Rabi knew that the true God, the Creator of all, had spoken these words, and he began to tremble. In tears he ran to his room. All of his pride, deception, arrogance and sin came before his eyes. He wanted to tell God how sorry he was for his evil actions, especially for stealing worship that belonged to God alone. He entered a period of crisis.

"Day after day, I, who had once thought myself on the verge of self-realization, now grovelled in abject self-condemnation. I thought of all the cigarettes I had stolen, the lies I had told, the proud and selfish life I had lived and the hatred in my heart towards my aunt and others. There had been times when I had even wished her dead, while at the same time preaching non-violence. My good deeds could never outweigh my bad deeds on any honest scale. I now feared the astral travel and the spirit visitations I had once exulted in, yet I knew no other way to search for God than through Yoga. My religion, my training, my experience in meditation had all taught me that only by looking within myself could I find truth, so I tried it again. The search

18

within, however, proved futile. Instead of finding God, I only stirred up a nest of evil that made me even more aware of my own heart's corruption. My misery only became greater, my sense of guilt and shame a burden impossible to bear."

About this time Rabi met a Christian called Molli. He discovered that she had once been a devout Hindu who claimed to have found true forgiveness, peace and love through turning to Jesus Christ as the only true God. At first Rabi was angry with this Hindu apostate, but as she gently spoke of the God she had come to know as Father, forgiver and provider, and of Jesus Christ who had died for all her sin and guilt and who had given her power to live a life that pleased God, something began to happen to Rabi.

"I wanted her peace and joy, but I was not going to give up any part of my religion! She hadn't said anything about that, but I could see that if I believed that Jesus was God and that He had died for me and could forgive my sins, then everything I had lived for as a Hindu was meaningless."

After half a day's discussion Molli left, but not before challenging Rabi to get on his knees before retiring to bed and ask God to show him the truth. Then, with a wave of her hand she was gone. Alone on his knees that evening Rabi, who had sought self-realization for so long, now realised he was hopelessly lost. The words of his Uncle came back to him when he described the Hindu priesthood:

"They talk a lot about self-realization but only become more selfish!"

Three weeks later, Rabi's cousin Krishna showed him a Bible and pointed to the words of Jesus in John chapter 3 verse 3, *"Unless a man is born again, he cannot see the kingdom of God."* Rabi, as he read the context, understood that Jesus was not talking about reincarnation but a spiritual birth that makes someone new.

"In the past I had sought mystical experiences as an escape from daily life, which Hindu philosophy called maya, an illusion. Now I wanted the power to face life, to live the life God had planned for me. I wanted to experience a deep change in what I was, not merely the superficial peace I felt during meditation which forsook me the moment I lost my temper. I needed to be born again, spiritually not physically."

The day finally came when Rabi's cousin invited him to a church meeting to hear about Jesus Christ. The preacher, a former Muslim, clearly presented the fact that every person in the world is a sinner by nature and by practice, and that the death of God's Son Jesus Christ on the cross is the only ransom price that God will accept in order to secure personal forgiveness for those willing to turn from their sin and receive Jesus as Lord of their life. Rabi wept tears of repentance for the way he had lived - for his anger, hatred, selfishness and pride, for the idols he had served and for accepting worship that belonged to God alone. He realised that Jesus wasn't just another god among millions, but was in fact the only true creator God who had loved him enough to become man and die for his sins. The Lord revealed the great truth of the atonement to Rabi – he saw by faith that *"Christ died for me!"* With that realization, fears of darkness lifted and light flooded his soul. He was born again.

Astral travel to other planets, unearthly music, psychedelic colours, Yogic visions and higher states of consciousness now appeared like dust and ashes. The new birth through Christ was not just another psychic trip. Rabi knew on the authority of the Bible that God had forgiven his sins. Never had he been so genuinely joyful as tears of repentance turned to tears of joy.

"For the first time in my life I knew what real peace was. That wretched, unhappy, miserable feeling left me. I was in communion with God and I knew it. I was one of God's children now. I had been born again."

Since his conversion to Jesus Christ in 1962, many of Rabi's relatives have become Christians too. Through the written and spoken word his remarkable story has spread throughout the world. He now warns that Hindu philosophy is spreading through Western culture in the form of mind-altering drugs, Yoga, self-help seminars and the New Age movement and that the gods he used to worship are demons deceiving millions of unsuspecting seekers. His message is unpalatable to many but unerringly true: *"There can be no mixing of Hinduism and Christianity. Jesus Christ alone is the answer to mankind's spiritual need."*

Three verses from the New Testament make this clear:

"Neither is there salvation in any other, for there is none other Name under heaven, given among men, whereby we must be saved." (Acts 4:12)

"There is one God and one mediator between God and men, the man Christ Jesus, who gave Himself a ransom for all." (1 Tim 2:5-6)

Jesus said, *"I am the way, the truth and the life. No man comes unto the Father but by Me."* (John 14:6)

CHAPTER 3

Self-Realization

R. Raghu
India

Raghu was born into an orthodox Brahmin family in one of the villages of central Tamil Nadu, the oldest child and only son in his family. His grandfather and great grandfathers had pioneered a famous school for religious studies in that village under the blessing of Sankaracharya Matt of Kancheepuram. A keen student of Hinduism, he participated willingly in all his family's rituals and frequently visited various temples.

At School he studied Sanskrit and learned the religious slokas. On becoming a Brahmachari he commenced the study of the Vedas, Vedanta and Upashinad under teachers of the Veda Padashala. His teachers initiated him into all the rituals necessary for him eventually to become a Shastri and advised him not to keep company with the low-caste people at his school.

After finishing school he proceeded to college for his higher education where, through the influence of Communism and Dravidianism, he began to question Hinduism for the first time. His forefathers belonged to the sect of Mandrikas (diviners who practise magic and predict the future). Though he allowed himself the luxury of developing a rebellious attitude towards Hinduism, because of his strong religious upbringing he found it impossible to completely reject his family's religion.

22

After completing his education he journeyed to Bombay in search of employment, initially lodging with his uncle. He took up writing articles and after succeeding in having them published in various magazines adopted a proud lifestyle and became a nuisance to his uncle. Asked to move out, Raghu rented a room elsewhere. His lack of career success made him wonder if perhaps he should drop his communistic leanings and return to the fold of Hinduism. Hoping the gods would prosper him, Raghu began to consume Hindu books. He devoured the Puranas, the Ramayana and the Bhavagad Gita. With his newly discovered breadth of expertise in Hindu teachings, together with his practice of TM, Yoga and the yagyas, Raghu began to attract admirers who bowed before him and sought his blessings. He soon began earning money from the offerings of his growing band of devotees.

One day Raghu caught sight of the world-famous guru Bhagwan Shree-Rajneesh. A huge crowd had gathered at the central railway station in Bombay to see him off. As Raghu saw many falling at the feet of Rajneesh a desire for fame and adulation was kindled in his heart. Before he could attain to such heights he felt he needed more knowledge, so he expanded his reading base to include a wide range of philosophical works.

At the invitation of his boss, Raghu agreed to attend a Bahai meeting. Liking what he heard and being assured that he could study the Bahai faith without having to leave his own religion, Raghu added numerous Bahai books to his ever growing reading list. With his mind firmly fixed on making money through knowledge, he even made regular visits to the Theosophical Society. Then he asked his secretary to supply him with a Bible. When he began to read it he was surprised to find animal sacrifices and other rituals practised by the Jewish people in the Old Testament. He concluded that these similarities between the Bible and Hinduism probably indicated that all religions were essentially the same and led to the same destination. The Old Testament stories fascinated him. He even modified and reinterpreted them in own his writings and promoted the idea that Jesus is just a messenger of God.

Although he didn't really realise it at the time, Raghu was searching for something. He pursued Yoga up to Kundalini Yoga but was warned against taking it further by his master. Raghu had hoped that meditation would fill the emptiness he felt in his heart, yet it failed. He spent his evenings listening to music and going to the cinema. He travelled to numerous holy places in India yet neither his knowledge, his money, his pleasures nor his fame could satisfy him.

December 1979 brought Raghu a precious opportunity. He decided to travel to the state of Tamil Nadu and meditate for three days until he received enlightenment. This would surely prove to be the turning point in his life. From there he could progress to the status of a guru. Full of hope and holy expectation Raghu made the journey to a desert country where day after day he sat and meditated, but nothing happened. The precious time ebbed away but the enlightenment he so earnestly sought and expected never came. Disappointed and frustrated, a shaken Raghu wondered why the gods were silent.

Towards the end of his stay, after another fruitless day, he returned downhearted and depressed to his hotel room. Sitting alone, his mind in turmoil, he regretted having wasted his time by coming to this place. While preparing to leave, the pressure within seemed to reach breaking point. He was so angry at himself and the world that literally felt like breaking the window of the hotel. At that moment he decided to sit down and think through his situation. As he went back in his mind over his fruitless search for fulfilment, suddenly a verse he had read in the Bible came to him;

"Jesus answered and said...Whoever drinks of this water shall thirst again, but whoever drinks of the water that I shall give him shall never thirst; but the water that I shall give him shall be in him a well of water springing up into everlasting life."

Where did that verse come from? What did it mean? Why had he suddenly recalled it? Then another verse came to him; *"All have sinned and come short of the glory of God."* No, Raghu thought, I am a Brahmin, I am not a sinner. I am holy and pure. What about all the Karmas I have been through in the past? Yet another verse answered his objections; *"If we say that we have no sin we deceive ourselves and the truth is not in us."*

A battle began to rage in Raghu's heart. The crucial moment of self-realization had finally come, but it was of a totally different nature to that which he had expected. Raghu finally acknowledged that he had been living in denial all along. He had been deceiving himself. The fact was, in the sight of a holy God he stood condemned as a guilty sinner. Raghu, a Brahmin who had blessed so many people and was revered by the crowds, came to an end of himself and his self-righteousness. He knew he had to confess his sin to God and humble himself in the dust. His thoughts went to the cross and what happened there to the Lord Jesus on account of his sin. Although Raghu did not realise it, God's Holy Spirit was working in his heart to draw him to Christ.

After a long struggle Raghu finally knelt down on the floor. He cried out to God, *"God, I am a sinner, I am a sinner. Please forgive me. Jesus Christ, I believe that You are God and that You died for me on the cross. Give me life. Quench my thirst. Save me!"*

He repeated the same words over and over but after a while he slowed up and a realization came over him that the burden, pressure and turmoil within had ceased. He knew peace for the first time in his life. Tears began to flow. He experienced a double realization; that he was a guilty sinner and that Christ has died and risen again to save him from his sins.

He returned to Bombay in January 1980, visiting his parents at Madurai. As he explained his experience of salvation they looked at him with justified scepticism. Raghu had tried so many different things before that they had learnt not to take him too seriously. However, by 1981 Raghu had been baptised and was regularly meeting with Christians for Bible study and fellowship. On meeting his parents a second time they questioned him more closely. Raghu confessed that he believed the God of the Bible was the only true God. He explained that all nationalities and castes are equally condemned before a holy God as sinners and need salvation through the Lord Jesus.

His father grew angry; "*How can I lift up my head now in our community when the son in whom I had such hopes, that one day he would be a guru, has now become a Christian, has broken caste and has turned away from his father's religion and the gods of his ancestors.*"

Rejected and pronounced dead by his family, Raghu 'the traitor' became an outcast. His followers felt he had let them down. "*What avatar* [incarnation] *is this? Please explain to us.*" Raghu tried to point them to His Saviour the Lord Jesus, but no one was willing to listen.

So Raghu began a new life. Eventually he rose to a good position in a large company in India but God had other plans! In 1984 he married a Christian lady called Lydia and felt the call of God to serve Him full-time as an evangelist in the regions of Sikkim, West Bengal, and also in the country of Nepal. Several churches have been formed there as the Lord has been pleased to bless his efforts and the work continues to this day.

26

CHAPTER 4

My Journey To Damascus

Dr. Uma Mahesh Bandarupalli
India

As recently as 1995 I was a staunch Hindu from a Brahmin family. It is hard for me to comprehend the change that has taken place in my life! I was born into an orthodox Brahmin family in 1978, becoming a guru by the age of 17. I am the second son of Seetha Rama Rao and Jayaprada Bandarupalli. My parents were both hardworking people. My father often went on overseas assignments for a leading public sector company (BHEL). Being the youngest in the family I enjoyed a great deal of freedom, the onus always falling on my older brother. Education in India is very competitive and I worked hard to keep ahead of my peers.

A German gentleman once asked me to explain the meaning of the first sloka from the Bhagavad-Gita. Sadly up until then religion had been very low on my list of priorities so I didn't know the answer to his question. I felt embarrassed that I could not answer him and that this Westerner had a greater interest in my scriptures than I did. The effect of this small incident was to produce in me an urge to master all of the Hindu scriptures. Suddenly I no longer found my academic life a chore. I now possessed an inward drive to assimilate every facet of Hinduism.

Unexpectedly at this time my father went to Saudi Arabia as an engineer to commission a power plant and I had to go with him. I was forced for two and a half years to learn the Koran. I had to learn Arabic and Islamic culture. I did not enjoy the experience at all and took the first opportunity I could to flee back to India. Once on home soil again, I re-immersed myself in Hinduism. My friends in the Gulf thought I was a fool for leaving the comforts of Saudi Arabia but I loved my country and religion more than human comforts. Besides, I felt that the Islamic law of the land treated all non-muslins as barbarians!

From childhood Sanskrit had been my second language. Being able to read and write in Sanskrit helped me immensely as I studied various Hindu texts under the guidance of my grand father who ran a Vedic school. I gradually evolved into a sanctimonious, modern yet fundamentalist Hindu. As I was taught that all other faiths are dangerous, I grew especially to dislike Christians who claimed that Jesus Christ is the only way to God. Dislike turned to hatred as I read accounts of what 'Christian Britain' had done to my country. 200 years of slavery and proselytization had led my land into poverty, chaos and division. I remained proud of my ancient superior religious culture. As far as I was concerned, the only Indian Christians were converts from the outcasts and untouchables.

During my time at pre-medical school I stayed with my grandmother. While there I was ordained as a special priest who could perform several exclusive rites and rituals. I was chosen to serve as a priest and Vedic teacher and started teaching at the local Vedic school. My specialties were the Upanishads and Sankaracharya's work.

Throughout my time at the school I made sure that I left all the Christians I met either crying or offended. I felt special antipathy towards Roman Catholics. They complained about my 'idolatry' but they had numerous idols themselves not to mention rites and rituals; and what about all the different denominations among Christians that were so different yet all claimed an exclusive hold on 'the truth'?

My increasing hatred for Christians was only matched by my increasing appetite for higher offices within Hinduism. I rose to the status of one who could perform marriages and yagas. I was chosen to represent the community in performing Chandi-yaga, which is performed before Dussera, a popular Hindu festival. I also developed a thorough knowledge of occult sciences like palmistry, astrology, and even Hatha Yoga. All of this made me very popular, gaining me the name 'Chinna Baba' (small guru). People would come from neighbouring villages and seek my counsel for their lives. They would wash my feet and sprinkle the ablutions on their heads. I was treated like a demi-god and was expected in time to become a Vedic teacher and a priest, though I was still quite young.

Things changed again and I gained admission into medical school, moving to the city of Hyderabad. I continued my priesthood at a religious learning centre there called Shanker Mutt and finally attained the status of guru. People began treating me like a king and my parents became known by my name. During these days my anti-Christian bias continued to dominate my life. I associated with a group of Hindu fundamentalists who planned to put down evangelical Christians by whatever method. I was present at some of their planning meetings where we identified several ways to isolate and persecute anyone who preached the gospel. Yet despite winning many arguments with Christian class-mates through the sheer power of my will and personality, they refused to retaliate. Their demeanour was always gracious even when I hurled abuse at them. This impressed me!

"Do you have a personal relationship with God?" a class-mate asked.

For the first time in my life I was speechless. The genuineness of the question and the sincerity of my friend made me give the matter serious thought. While I had had many emotional and euphoric experiences, and I knew just exactly what ritual needed to be performed on every occasion and in every situation, and I knew that God existed as a 'supreme spirit' - yet all of this was mere head knowledge, not the personal relationship my class-mate had asked me about.

My embarrassment led to anger and frustration. Ultimately all these experiences led me to a pivotal decision. I decided to prove that the supreme authority of all Christians is but a collection of lies. I took on the Bible itself! To preserve my reputation as a Christian hater, I avoided reading the Bible at home. I secretly walked three miles each evening after classes from my medical school to the state regional library in order to read the Bible. There in a quiet corner of the library I began to read Matthew's Gospel, the first book of the New Testament. The first few pages were historical but when I reached chapter 5 I read these words:

"And seeing the multitudes, Jesus went up into a mountain: and when He was set, His disciples came unto Him: and He opened His mouth, and taught them, saying,

> *'Blessed are the poor in spirit: for theirs is the kingdom of heaven.*
> *'Blessed are they who mourn: for they shall be comforted.*
> *'Blessed are the meek: for they shall inherit the earth.*
> *'Blessed are they who hunger and thirst after righteousness:*
> *for they shall be filled.*
> *'Blessed are the merciful: for they shall obtain mercy.*

'Blessed are the pure in heart: for they shall see God.
'Blessed are the peacemakers: for they shall be called
the children of God.
'Blessed are they who are persecuted for righteousness' sake: for theirs
is the kingdom of heaven.
'Blessed are you, when men shall revile you, and persecute you, and
shall say all manner of evil against you falsely, for My sake'."

At first the words of Jesus sounded common enough. 'Meekness, holiness and poverty' are common themes in all religions, especially Hinduism. But as I continued to read I began to feel as if Jesus was talking to me, rather than me simply reading His words. I started to take His message personally. Quickly I realised that I possessed none of the qualities He outlined as essential for admission into the Kingdom of God. Under this kind of pressure I would ordinarily have fought back, but I felt as if someone far superior to me was weighing me up and I had fallen short of His standards. Feeling somewhat crestfallen I decided to move on but I couldn't get away from Jesus' words. I had always viewed myself as virtuous and holy in the eyes of the community, but suddenly a new and disturbing thought invaded my mind. Could it be that I was a sinner?

Another shock lay ahead. The Bible clearly condemned idolatry as a serious sin. If that was true I was easily one of the worst idolaters in the world. I began to feel very uneasy. I believed that my culture and religion were unquestionably great. Yet big questions confronted me. For example, if God is spirit, as most religions claim, how can man give form or shape to that spirit and mould it into an image? Spirit by definition has no form. I also knew from my studies that my own Hindu scriptures contained some material that classified idolatry as a sin. (Less that 1% of Hindus know this fact because today's Hinduism has lost its connection with its Vedic roots).

31

Still, I could not tolerate the thought of being a sinner. In my turmoil I threw away the Bible and tried to forget the whole idea but I could not erase the thoughts from my mind. I felt haunted and restless. Then an old Indian saying came back to me, 'a diamond can be cut only by another diamond'. I decided to do a comparative study of my Hindu scriptures and the Bible. I visited the Adigranthalay (Library of Ancient Manuscripts) in Hyderabad and commenced my task. I spent long nights studying Hinduism from scratch. I started to come across numerous contradictions. Take the famous Advaita theory for example. It states that man and God are one (see the Yagnyavalkya Upanishad). Yet this is denounced in the Brihadaranyaka Upanishad where I discovered that man's sin will always keep him separate from God (Dvaita). I found scores of such contradictions, but the most important discovery I made concerned the status of Jesus Christ. It became clear to me that He could not be just a great moral teacher - He had to be God!

The more I read the Bible, the more settled my mind became. I slowly began emerging out of mythology and into truth. Though I had concluded that Jesus was God, I still could not bring myself to wholeheartedly acknowledge the fact that Jesus was *my Lord*. Yet I could plainly see my hopeless condition as a sinner and the impossibility of cleansing myself or bringing myself to God. The Bible made my helpless situation abundantly clear:

"By the deeds of the law there shall no flesh be justified in His sight: for by the law is the knowledge of sin. But now the righteousness of God without the law is manifested, being witnessed by the law and the prophets; even the righteousness of God which is by faith of Jesus Christ unto all and upon all those who believe: for there is no difference: for all have sinned, and come short of the glory of God; being justified freely by his grace through the redemption that is in Christ Jesus: Whom God has set forth to be a propitiation through faith in His blood, to declare His righteousness for the

remission of sins that are past, through the forbearance of God." (Romans 3:19-24)

The Bible declares that the Lord Jesus offered Himself as a holy sacrifice on the cross, shedding His precious blood that mankind might be cleansed from sin. The penalty that was due to sinners was paid through the death of the Lord Jesus Christ. Although *"the wages of sin are death,"* because of the offering of Christ, *"the gift of God is eternal life through Jesus Christ our Lord"* (Romans 6:23). On the third day after His death Jesus rose again having conquered sin and death. Yet, despite knowing all of this truth, I still found it agonisingly difficult to fully own my sinfulness and need of this Saviour.

I continued to study the Bible for many months. My studies finally compelled me to stop worshipping idols, much to the displeasure of my family. Then the annual Hindu festival of Maha Shivaratri came around. I was in the habit of performing special rituals at the local temple during this special family time and consequently my family saw this as a test of my loyalty to Hinduism. I had resolved in my mind that, having learnt the truth, if I continued to ignore it I was worse than the beast of the field (this I learnt from the wisdom of Kalidas, the great poet). So, for the first time in my life I prayed in simple words to God:

"God, if you can see my plight, please get me out of this somehow. I do not want to go to the temple."

In the mercy of God I developed a very high temperature and my family decided that I was too ill to attend the festival. After my family left the house I found myself all alone with my thoughts. As I lay on my bed, I was suddenly overcome by deep anguish. God reminded me of all the different ways in which I had sinned against Him. My pride, hatred, deeds of persecution and idolatry played out in my mind like a film. At last my self-righteousness broke and from my heart I truly accepted my sinful lost condition. I clearly saw and agreed that I deserved the consequences of my sin - death and hell. Through my tears and confession of guilt I called out to the Lord Jesus to forgive my sins. I let go of everything I had trusted in up to that point and simply rested in the Lord Jesus Christ and the work He did on the cross for me. I clearly saw that Jesus took my place on the cross and bore the punishment due to my sins. I simply reached out and made salvation my own by faith. That night the Lord saved me from my sins and the eternal torment of hell. He gave me peace and joy such as I had never known in all my life and through all my previous experiences.

"For God so loved the world, that He gave His only begotten Son, that whosoever believeth in Him should not perish, but have everlasting life." (John 3:16)

The world is full of myths, legends and fables that claim to lead people to salvation but all of them are of human origin. Jesus Christ alone is God's answer to our need as seen in the wonderful love He displayed on the cross by giving Himself a ransom for our sin.

"Neither is there salvation in any other: for there is none other name under heaven given among men, whereby we must be saved." (Acts 4:12)

"Jesus said unto him, 'I am the way, the truth, and the life: no man comes unto the Father, but by Me'." (John 14:6)

From the moment I became a follower of Christ, the difficulties I faced were formidable. I was suddenly treated as an untouchable. Those who despised me sometimes hit me and even spat in my face. I was shunned at home and at medical school but

34

God helped me through every circumstance. My previous associations with Hindu fundamentalists led to attempts on my life as they accused me of being a traitor. By God's grace I not only survived all of these events but have been able to move on and now have a wonderful family of my own. I sincerely urge you to consider your life in the light of the truth of Jesus Christ, truth that can transform a repentant believing sinner into one who enjoys a pure, holy and meaningful life.

"If you will confess with your mouth that Jesus is Lord, and believe in your heart that God has raised him from the dead, you will be saved." (Romans 10:9)

CHAPTER 5

Christ is
The Answer

Sadhu Chellappa
India

Sadhu Chellappa's grandfather, a well-known guru, died when Sadhu was ten. In the years that followed Sadhu continued to grow up in a traditional Brahmin family in India, receiving schooling in the Vedic scriptures in a Hindu temple during World War 2.

The Brahmins form the highest ranking of the four social classes in Hindu India. The privileged status of the Brahmins can be traced back to the late Vedic period, when the Indo-European-speaking settlers in northern India were already divided into four classes or varnas. Brahmins or priests composed the first class. The second class consisted of warriors (called the Kshatriya class). Traders made up the third class (called the Vaisya class) which left the fourth class for the labourers (called the Sudra class). Since those early days there has been little change in the Brahmins' position. The 21st century still sees them enjoying great prestige and many privileges, though their claim to *actual* privileges is no longer officially recognized at either legal or governmental levels. Brahmins believe that they are inherently of greater ritual purity than members of other castes and that only they are capable of performing certain essential rituals and ceremonies. Since the study and recitation of the sacred scriptures has always been the preserve of the spiritual elite, all Indian scholarship has rested in the hands of the Brahmins for many centuries. One such privileged Brahmin child, Sadhu Chellappa, recalls his upbringing:

"I never had academic studies but was left in the Vedic classes where I had a guru as my teacher, through whom I memorised the scriptures without understanding their meaning at first. As I began a journey that I expected one day would lead to me becoming a guru, the first thing I learnt was the confession of sin. I was taught a particular set of statements in Sanskrit which I was expected to recite every time I prayed. How well I remember its solemn tone:

'I am born in sin; I am a doer of sin; I am a sinful self, so I am a sinner. I covet sin through my mind; I covet sin through my looking; I covet sin through my body and I covet sin through my tongue...God save me from all kinds of sin.'

"I was not taught to which of the 300 million gods of India this prayer was addressed but I recited it many, many times. The constant repetition of this prayer, combined with a growing realization of my constant inward propensity to sin as a human being, led me to develop a desire to be rid of my sin. I decided to ask my guru about my problem. He said, *'It is impossible. It would involve you taking many, many rebirths.'*

'How many rebirths?' I asked

'Thousands,' he said.

The religions of Hinduism, Jainism, Buddhism and Sikhism, all of which originated in India, teach the doctrine of karma (meaning 'act'), otherwise known as the law of cause and effect. Sadhu was taught from his childhood that every act one does in this present life has its effect in the next. The soul's process of transmigration through the wheel of births and rebirths (samsara) will prove to be endless unless one achieves salvation (moksha) through enlightenment, the moment at which the individual soul (atman) becomes one with the absolute soul (Brahman). To continue Sadhu's story:

"I asked my guru what I was in my former life that had caused my suffering as a man in this life. I wanted to know what I had done wrong so that I could put it right between God and myself. In response my guru told me to study one of the Upanishads. In this Hindu scripture there is a beautiful story about a disciple and his Master who talk together. The disciple asks, *'Master, tell me what I was in my former birth, what I am in this birth and what I will be in my future birth?'*

"The guru answers with a story. He says; *'A small boy caught a butterfly and tried to pull off its wings and legs. A man warned him, 'You naughty boy, if you do this you will be born as a butterfly and this butterfly will be born as a boy and will pull off your wings and legs.' The boy answered: 'No, Master, I might have been a butterfly in my former life; the butterfly might have been a boy pulling off my wings and legs; that is why I'm taking revenge in this life.' The Master answered: 'I do not know what I was, neither what I shall be, but I know what I am now. If I do not find the way of salvation in this life, what is the use of giving birth in thousands of lives.'*

"The story ended with that quotation. It at once shook my faith in reincarnation while at the same time bringing joy to my heart. I felt convinced by this scripture that reincarnation was illogical and the idea of being born again and again could not be true. Interestingly I have since discovered that the teaching of reincarnation is not actually found in the earlier Hindu scriptures.

The same can be said for many of the gods and goddesses in Hinduism. I asked my guru, *'Why should I worship all these gods and goddesses whose names are not written in the Scriptures? How did they come into existence?'* But the more questions I asked the more angry he became with me. To be honest, my one desire was simply to understand Hinduism properly and profess my faith as a real son of a priest. My grandfather had been a learned man in Sanskrit, but unfortunately he had died, so I could not go to him with my questions. How I regretted his passing. I had to search from guru to guru. What else could I do? In their exasperation some of them claimed I was becoming an atheist.

"My questions finally became so incessant that I was asked to leave the Vedic scripture class. As a consequence my family also rejected me. My excommunication from the temple was an acute embarrassment and abomination to them. When they told me to leave home, I had no option but to live on the streets for a while. My circumstances proved to be most trying and I passed through many difficulties.

"Even though I eventually married and had children (through my uncle's intervention), I still ended up going downhill morally. The fears of my gurus seemed to come true as I did indeed toy with atheism for a while. I eventually turned to drinking, gambling and other forms of sin. I borrowed money from people I could not repay, which landed me in the law courts. Due to my folly and irresponsible behaviour my children often went without food and my wife led a miserable life. What pain she bore in her heart as a result of my reckless lifestyle.

"While travelling on a train one day, I decided that life was not worth living and considered jumping out and killing myself. My privileged Brahmin upbringing, my devout Hindu training and all my knowledge of the ancient scriptures seemed powerless to help me at that moment. I was in total despair with nowhere to turn. As I reached the door I heard a distant voice through a loudspeaker quoting from the Bible, '*He who conceals his sin shall not prosper.*'

"I was stunned by the clarity and directness of the quotation. It was not a verse I ever remembered reading. I presumed it must be a scripture from another holy book, so I got off at the next station and walked back along the railway line to find out more. Eventually I came across what I instantly recognized as a Christian gathering. I had been told that Christianity belonged to Western people and that Jesus Christ was a Westerner. As far as India was concerned I believed that the only Indian Christians belonged to the low caste, considered untouchable by a Brahmin like me. Thus when I reached the place I stood alone under a tree some way off but within earshot. The preacher was talking about sin. He related how that one Hindu saint cried out to God, '*Lord, just as a calf is bound by a strong rope, so am I bound by sin. How can I escape from the punishment of sin?*' Surely this is the agonising cry of all the Hindu saints in India who do not understand that God has been manifested in flesh (Jesus Christ) and offered Himself as a sacrifice for their sins.

"After explaining that sin leads to eternal punishment in hell the preacher stated, '*There is a way of salvation.*' I listened more carefully as he spoke about how Jesus Christ the Son of God came into this world through the virgin birth and lived a sinless life. He told how Jesus wore a crown of thorns and shed His blood on the cross as He gave His life for sinners, before rising again from the dead three days later. I felt this was the answer I needed, so swallowing my pride I approached the man and asked him if I could have this Jesus as my Saviour so that my many sins could be forgiven. The preacher took me aside to speak with a Christian philosopher who was accompanying him.

"After three hours of talking with me he wanted me to 'receive Christ' immediately, but I wanted to learn more before making such a momentous decision. He gave me a Bible and told me to take it home and read it. At about eleven o'clock that night I opened the Bible at random and saw the words, *'He who rejects Me, and does not receive My words, has that which judges him; the word that I have spoken will judge him in the last day'* (John 12:48). I closed the Bible in surprise. If the word was going to judge me, why should I continue to read it? Perhaps I could avoid the judgment by not reading it!

"In the morning I opened it again and started at the beginning. I read of the creation of the world: *'In the beginning God created the heavens and the earth'* (Genesis 1:1). I continued a few chapters and came upon the record of Noah's flood. The flood made sense to me because in the Indian scriptures, as in the books of many ancients cultures, it is also recorded that the world was once flooded. When I came to the books of Exodus and Leviticus I felt on familiar ground because I recognized shades of my sacrificial Hindu culture there, with its priesthood, rituals, washings and holy ashes.

"However what was entirely new to me was what I discovered when I turned to the New Testament book called 'Hebrews'. There I learnt that Jesus was the *fulfilment* of all the animal sacrifices that had preceded Him. I realized that Jesus' sacrifice on the cross was a once-for-all, never to be repeated offering to end all offerings. I found out that in Christ all the previous sacrifices have come to an end. He is the one true sin-offering, the value of which stands for ever. Let me quote what the Bible actually says:

"*And every priest stands ministering daily and offering repeatedly the same sacrifices, which can never take away sins. But this Man* [Jesus

41

Christ], *after He had offered one sacrifice for sins forever, sat down at the right hand of God, from that time waiting till His enemies are made His footstool. For by one offering He has perfected forever those who are being sanctified.*" (Hebrews 10:11-14)

"The whole picture finally became clear. I was a lost sinner who deserved eternal judgment. Jesus was the perfect Saviour whose death satisfied God's eternal justice and provided salvation for me as a free gift. I turned from my sin at that moment and put my faith and trust in the risen Christ alone as my Lord and Saviour. I was born again instantly – I underwent a spiritual birth 'on the inside' as the Holy Spirit of God regenerated me, giving me new life and bringing me into a relationship with God Himself.

"When I told my parents that I now believed in Jesus Christ as my Lord and God, my father said, *'Don't come near our home!'* My mother told me never to come back again and my sisters also rejected me. Though rejected I clung on to a verse of scripture which reads, *'Believe on the Lord Jesus Christ, and you shall be saved, you and your household'* (Acts 16:31). Every day I used to put my finger on that scripture and claim it as a promise from God! The Lord graciously worked in my family so that within one year all of them had turned to the Lord too."

Since that time Sadhu Chellappa has served the Lord as a preacher of the gospel in India, and has been an instrument of blessing in the lives of many others by pointing them to the only Saviour of sinners, the Lord Jesus Christ.

CHAPTER 6

For the Reader

The Hindus in this book all shared a determination to discover the truth about God. The Bible promises that God always rewards those who seek Him with all their hearts, but who or what is God?

Most of the Hindu scriptures speak of God (Brahman) as being the universe itself: *"God is in truth the whole universe."* However, in order to know God, we must begin by understanding that He is actually the uncreated Creator of the universe. The Bible says: *"In the beginning God created the heavens and the earth"* (Genesis 1:1). He existed before creation and transcends all that He created. Though He alone is worthy of worship millions in our world today bow down to objects of wood and stone, worshipping creatures and creations rather than the Creator Himself. It is widely believed that monotheism is a recent development in religion, the more ancient religions being either polytheistic or animistic. However the Bible gives the opposite picture as it traces humanity's historical move away from the worship of the one true creator God to the worship of created things in the following remarkable passage:

"For the wrath of God is revealed from heaven against all ungodliness and unrighteousness of men, who suppress the truth in unrighteousness, because what may be known of God is manifest in them, for God has shown it to them. For since the creation of the world His invisible attributes are clearly seen, being understood by the things that are made, even His eternal

power and Godhead, so that they are without excuse; because, although they knew God, they did not glorify Him as God, nor were thankful, but became futile in their thoughts, and their foolish hearts were darkened. Professing to be wise, they became fools, and changed the glory of the incorruptible God into an image made like corruptible man, and birds, and four-footed animals and creeping things. Therefore God also gave them up to uncleanness, in the lusts of their hearts, to dishonour their bodies among themselves, who exchanged the truth of God for the lie, and worshipped and served the creature rather than the Creator, who is blessed forever. Amen." (Romans 1:18-25)

Humanity's fall away from true worship to creature worship – or even worse, the attempt to worship the true God *through* idols – is a sad story of rebellion, superstition and darkness. Yet in truth it is but one manifestation of a far greater underlying problem; the root problem of sin in the human heart. Far from being maya, an illusion, sin is a terrible reality. It is that inward bias toward rebellion and evil that has dwelt deep in the hearts of all mankind ever since the rebellion of our first parents Adam and Eve in the garden of Eden. "*By one man's disobedience many were made sinners*" (Romans 5:19).

As a result of their wilful choice to disobey God, all of humanity is afflicted by a fallen corrupt nature from birth – and sinners by nature soon become sinners by practice. We do what we do because we are what we are. Remember the prayer of the Brahmins: "*I am born in sin; I am a doer of sin; I am a sinful self, so I am a sinner. I covet sin through my mind; I covet sin through my looking; I covet sin through my body and I covet sin through my tongue.*" What is true of the Brahmins is true of all castes and creeds. The Bible, comparing Jews with Gentiles states: "*there is no difference, for all have sinned and fall short of the glory of God.*" (Romans 3:23) We have all missed God's righteous standards by a mile. Not only have we failed to do the duties of worship and service that God requires of us, but we have also deliberately broken His commandments

44

again and again. Have you ever told a lie? That makes you a liar. After all, how many murders make a man a murderer? Just one. Have you ever stolen anything, no matter how small? That makes you a thief. Have you ever lusted after someone who is not your husband or wife? That makes you an adulterer in your heart. Have you ever worshipped an image or a created thing rather than the Creator Himself? That makes you an idolater. The penalty for this kind of sinful rebellion in word, thought and deed is to be separated forever from God in the torment of hell.

When sincere religious people first realize they are sinners, their usual and understandable first reaction is to try and cleanse themselves from sin by every kind of charitable deed and religious act. Hindus try various forms of Yoga and good works to effect inner cleansing and freedom from the chains of sin but to no avail. Some, who attain what they believe is enlightenment, claim to have reached godhood and self-realization, but this is simply another form of idolatry – the worship of self.

True enlightenment begins by turning one's back on finding the answer within oneself or through one's own efforts and agreeing with God's assessment of the human condition in His word the Bible which says: "*We are all like an unclean thing, and all our righteousnesses* [good deeds] *are like filthy rags; we all fade as a leaf, and our iniquities, like the wind, have taken us away.*" (Isaiah 64:6)

Since we are helpless and guilty sinners we cannot hope to restore our relationship with a holy God by our own efforts. All that we do is tainted by our sinfulness and is therefore unacceptable to a righteous God. Would you trust in what the Bible calls a 'filthy rag' to bring you to God? No. True wisdom lies in humbling ourselves and bowing at the feet of our Creator acknowledging we are sinful and He is holy and just. Religious ritual and ceremony appeal to human pride, but as long as we feel we have the resources within ourselves, or that it lies within our own power to bring ourselves to God, we will never find the way. It's a hard lesson to learn and it goes against the grain, but it is the only true path to peace and rest.

Eternal life and personal salvation are available to all, but attainable by none through self-effort and religious works. Instead, God has provided the way for us to be reconciled to Himself through His Son, Jesus Christ. The Hebrew prophets, through God's Spirit, predicted the coming of this Saviour, hundreds of years before He was born. They foretold that He would:

- be born of a virgin, and so be without sin (Isaiah 7:14)
- be the Son of God, meaning God incarnate (Isaiah 9:6-7)
- be rejected by His own people (Isaiah 53)
- be crucified for our sins (Isaiah 53; Zechariah 12:10)
- be buried and raised from the dead (Psalm 16:10-11)
- ascend back to heaven (Psalm 68:18)
- return to the earth as the Judge of mankind (Zechariah 14).

These prophets were clearly talking about the coming of the Lord Jesus Christ, God the Son. God Himself took the form of a human being and lived a life of complete perfection free of sin. When Jesus Christ was crucified it was in order to bear our sins in His own body on the cross. He gave Himself as a ransom sacrifice on our behalf so that we could be brought into a personal relationship with God now and forever in heaven.

The work to accomplish your salvation and freedom from indwelling sin has already been done to perfection. When Jesus died on the cross He cried out *"It is finished"* (John 19:30). He was announcing that the work of salvation stood accomplished through His atoning sufferings and death on the cross. In the

46

Bible Jesus is called the *"Lord our Righteousness"* (Jeremiah 23:5-6). Once a sinner repents and believes on the Lord Jesus Christ, God declares that person to be righteous on the basis of the substitutionary death of Christ on his or her behalf. As proof that He was satisfied with the sacrifice of His Son as the perfect and complete offering for sin, God raised Jesus from the dead on the third day, and because Jesus rose again from the dead and ascended back to heaven, He can come and live in your heart today through God's Holy Spirit, if you will humble yourself and receive Him by faith.

In India millions of people look to the gurus to be their bridge to salvation, but the gurus themselves are sinners just like the rest of us. Only Jesus the Son of God, through His death and resurrection, has destroyed the power of sin, rendering God able to save and forgive all who come to Him in repentance and faith.

Listen to what Jesus says about Himself:

"I am the way, the truth and the life. No-one comes to the Father except by Me." (John 14:6)

"I am the door; if anyone enters through Me, he shall be saved." (Jn 10:9)

"I am the resurrection and the life; he who believes in Me shall live even if he dies." (John 11:25)

"I am the light of the world; he who follows Me shall not walk in darkness, but shall have the light of life." (John 8:12)

"For God so loved the world that He gave His only begotten Son that whoever believes in Him shall not perish, but have everlasting life." (John 3:16)

Why don't you humble yourself and turn to God today – forsake your idols, give up any thought of self-realization and believe that He died on the cross for your sin and rose again from the dead. This is the only way to true forgiveness and peace with God. Abandon your trust in everything else, including yourself, and trust your eternal salvation to the Lord Jesus Christ alone. Eternal life is a gift from God that you receive by faith and not by works (Romans 6:23). The good works you will do after becoming a believer in Christ will spring out of a deep sense of gratitude to Him for loving you and dying for you, not out of an attempt to become or stay a Christian.

"For by grace you have been saved through faith, and that not of yourselves; it is the gift of God, not of works, lest anyone should boast." (Ephesians 2:8-9)

If through this book you have trusted in the Lord Jesus Christ alone for your eternal salvation you should immediately take the following steps:

1. Thank Him for what He has done for you and ask yourself the question, "What can I now do for Him?"

2. Start speaking daily to Him in prayer from your heart, bringing Him praise and thanksgiving, as well as asking Him for blessings.

3. Obtain a Bible and start reading and studying it. It's best to begin with the Gospels (e.g. Mark or John) and read through the New Testament first before progressing to the Old Testament. Ask God to give you understanding as to how to apply the Bible's teachings practically to your life.

4. Find a Bible believing Church and regularly attend its meetings and be baptised.

5. Tell others what the Lord Jesus has done for you.

Acknowledgements:

1. The publisher for *Destined for Royalty* is unknown.
2. *Death of a Guru*, Copyright © 1984 by Dave Hunt and Rabi Maharaj. Published by Harvest House Publishers, Eugene, Oregon 97402, USA www.harvesthousepublishers.com
3. *Self Realization* supplied by Mr R. Raghu, Siliguri, West Bengal, India.
4. *My Journey to Damascus* supplied by Dr. M. Bandarupalli, Leicester, England.
5. *Christ is The Answer*, Copyright © 1996 by Sadhu Chellappa, Icthus Media Services, taken from his personal testimony on audio cassette.

Also available:

Dawn of the New Age	*5 New Agers Relate Their Search for the Truth*
Angels of Light	*5 Spiritualists Test the Spirits*
The Pilgrimage	*5 Muslims Make the Greatest Discovery*
Witches and Wizards	*5 Witches Find Eternal Wisdom*
They Thought They Were Saved	*5 Christians Recall a Startling Discovery*
Messiah	*5 Jewish People Make the Greatest Discovery*
Many Ways to God?	*5 Religious Leaders discover the truth*
The Evolution Crisis	*5 Evolutionists Think Again*

If you would like confidential help or further information, please feel free to contact us. We can supply free Bibles, literature and details of Bible believing churches in your area. If this book has been a help to you please let us know. We greatly value the feedback we receive from our readers.

Published by:

John Ritchie Ltd.
40 Beansburn, Kilmarnock, Ayrshire, KA3 1RL.
Tel: +44 (0) 1563 326394
Fax: +44 (0) 1563 571191
Email: sales@johnritchie.co.uk
Web: www.ritchiechristianmedia.co.uk